Lessons We Can Learn From The Animals

Eight Children's Sermons
And Activity Pages

Julia E. Bland

CSS Publishing Company, Inc., Lima, Ohio

LESSONS WE CAN LEARN FROM THE ANIMALS

*To all the children at
Ash Grove and Barnard, Kansas*

Copyright © 2001 by
CSS Publishing Company, Inc.
Lima, Ohio

The original purchaser may photocopy material in this publication for use as it was intended (i.e. worship material for worship use; educational material for classroom use; dramatic material for staging or production). No additional permission is required from the publisher for such copying by the original purchaser only. Inquiries should be addressed to: Permissions, CSS Publishing Company, Inc., P.O. Box 4503, Lima, Ohio 45802-4503.

Scripture quotations are from the *New Revised Standard Version of the Bible*, copyright 1989 by the Division of Christian Education of the National Council of the Churches of Christ in the USA. Used by permission.

ISBN: 0-7880-1809-4   PRINTED IN U.S.A.

Table Of Contents

Introduction And Suggestions From The Author   4

Children's Sermons

   Stubborn Mules   5
      Deuteronomy 30:19-20; John 3:16

   Roaring Lions   6
      Colossians 3:8; Proverbs 15:1

   Screaming Monkeys   7
      Colossians 4:6a; 1 Corinthians 10:31; Colossians 1:10

   Bossy Tigers   8
      Matthew 7:12; Romans 12:10

   Messy Raccoons   9
      Psalm 141:3; James 3:2-12; Psalm 19:14

   Crowing Roosters   10
      Philippians 2:3b; Matthew 20:28; Galatians 5:26

   Buggy Thinking   11
      Psalm 139:23-24; Philippians 2:5; Colossians 3:2; Proverbs 12:5a

   Funny Looking Animals   13
      Galatians 3:26-29; Colossians 3:10-11; James 2; Ephesians 2:14-15

Children's Activity Pages   15

Answer Keys   31

Introduction And Suggestions From The Author

The lessons given here are based on scripture. They are meant to help children know Jesus as their Lord and do as he asks by developing Christian character with good personal habits.

In this series we hope to have fun and to capture and keep the children's attention by rhyming words. Yet, the lessons themselves are all ones we need to work on.

The coloring side of the activity sheet will be the visual aid in each lesson. If you prefer not to hand them out ahead of time or during your presentation, you could copy an extra for yourself, color it, and mount it on construction paper. Have this to show and read during the lesson. Then, give the children their own copy when you are finished. This works better in some groups who tend to be distracted easily and might bother others by the rattling of their paper.

Each lesson has an activity sheet. One side is for young children to color and is also your visual aid. Older children will enjoy the word puzzles and games on the other side. Provide crayons and pencils for the children to take back to the pew with them.

Ask questions and give your children time to answer and get involved, but children can say unexpected things so be ready to lead them back to your subject. Always study the lesson and pray ahead of time.

These lessons were prepared for use during the morning worship hour, but may easily be used during other times of Christian education of children. Remember the promise of scripture found in Isaiah 55:11:

So shall my word be that goes out from my mouth;
it shall not return to me empty,
but it shall accomplish that which I purpose,
and succeed in the thing for which I sent it.

God will bless your efforts to teach the children.

Julia E. Bland

Stubborn Mules
Jesus asks us to let him be our Lord, love and obey him.

Scripture: Deuteronomy 30:19-20; John 3:16

Visual Aid: Use the coloring side of the activity page

Advance Preparations: Copy enough activity pages for each child to have one and have them ready to hand out.

The Sermon:
(*Hand out the activity pages, coloring side up.*) Here is a paper with pictures and rhyming words.

First I have a question for you. Do you know what it means to be stubborn? Someone is stubborn if they won't do something that they've been asked to do. Sometimes boys and girls are stubborn. Mom might say, "Pick up your toys" or "Clean your room." But it doesn't get done. Someone has been stubborn and won't do what they were asked to do. Mom might have to get tough! I hope you are never stubborn to your mom and dad.

Do you know anyone who makes it hard to do anything with them because they are stubborn? They won't play checkers, they won't play tag, they won't play ball, or they won't watch a program. They won't do anything they're asked. Sometimes when we talk about being stubborn, we say, "Stubborn as a mule." There's a little rhyme on your paper, but I don't think we are really talking about mules. See what you think.

> **If a mule says, "I won't do*
> *Anything you want me to,"*
> *Should I hit him or kick him,*
> *Make faces and shout?*
> *Should I pinch him, or trip him,*
> *Or sit down and pout?*

What do you think? Should we do any of these things? We shouldn't do any of these things because we can't make anyone do something, even though we'd like to very much.

God doesn't make anyone do as he wants them to either. God has given each of us the freedom to make our own choices. The greatest choice we'll ever make is to choose Jesus as our Lord and Savior. And when we do, we choose to love and obey him, to do what he has told us. God hopes we will do that, but he doesn't make us. Some words from Deuteronomy in the Bible say: "... I have set before you life and death ... Choose life ... loving the Lord your God, obeying him, and holding fast to him." Jesus asks us to believe in him, obey him as our Lord, and if we will, he will give us eternal life. That means a happy life now and forever (John 3:16).

Let us never be stubborn to Jesus. But there is a time when it is good to be stubborn. How can that be? We need to be stubborn and say, "No," if ever we are asked to do something that we know is wrong and would not please Jesus. Those wrong things will only cause unhappiness.

I hope you'll always choose Jesus and never be stubborn to him and what he asks you to do.

*Use visual aid

Roaring Lions
Jesus asks us to use kind, soft words.

Scripture: Colossians 3:8; Proverbs 15:1

Visual Aid: Use the coloring side of the activity page

Advance Preparations: Copy enough activity pages for each child to have one and have them ready to hand out.

The Sermon:
(*Hand out the activity pages coloring side up.*) Have you ever been to a zoo? Did you ever see a lion? Did you ever hear a lion roar? They are very loud. Sometimes they even scare the other animals in the zoo when they roar.

*This paper has a picture of a lion and some rhyming words. Let's see if it is really about lions.

If a lion wants to roar,
Should we let it in the door?

Roaring's like a bad disease.
Anyone can hatch it.
It spreads throughout the whole household.
Be careful or you'll catch it.

If you roar at me,
I'll roar at you.
We'll wake the baby,
And she roars too.

Then Mom comes to see.
She adds her roars.
Oh, we should have kept
That lion outdoors!

It might be that we are not talking about lions, but about boys and girls and moms and dads.

If someone says or does something we don't like, what do we do? Do we sometimes yell and roar at them? This is especially easy at home with sisters and brothers. If they use our crayons or our toys, we don't like it and we yell. We roar about it. Or maybe they won't share with us and that makes us roar. Then what happens? They roar back! And before we know it, Mom or Dad is roaring at us both for roaring. Sometimes they have to roar to get our attention.

Did you ever have a bad cold or some disease? It's easy to spread the germs of the cold or disease to others in our family. Roaring can be like that too. Roaring spreads and causes unhappy, hurt feelings. Why is it so easy to roar?

Maybe it's because we are all a little selfish and are concerned more about our feelings and what we want than we should be. What we want and how we feel is so important that it causes us to roar about it. God's people should be careful. Listen to what the Bible says in Colossians 3:8: "But now you must get rid of all such things — anger, wrath, malice, slander, and abusive language from your mouth." So you see? God is not pleased with loud, angry words. What shall we do? Proverbs 15:1 has a good suggestion (see it there on your paper): *"A soft answer turns away wrath, but a harsh word stirs up anger." This will be hard. Can we give a soft answer to someone who roars at us? Let's don't stop trying.

*Use visual aid

Screaming Monkeys
Jesus asks us to have good manners.

Scripture: Colossians 4:6a; 1 Corinthians 10:31-32a; Colossians 1:10

Visual Aid: Use the coloring side of the activity page

Advance Preparations: Copy enough activity pages for each child to have one and have them ready to hand out.

The Sermon:
(*Hand out the activity pages, coloring side up.*) Here we are again. Another paper with a rhyme. This time there are pictures of monkeys.

> *Should monkeys scream
> for ice cream?

I don't think this paper is about monkeys at all. I think it's about boys and girls and maybe moms and dads. What are we talking about? Do you ever scream for ice cream? Perhaps for a certain toy you'd like? Or yelled to go to the park, swimming, or a friend's house? Maybe to watch a movie? I hope not. Yet, we all sometimes forget to use good manners. Let's read again:

> *There is a word, PLEASE.
> And if they'll use it,
> I doubt if anyone
> Will refuse it.

Sometimes the answer to what we want will be, "No," even if we say, "Please," but we will have done as we should by using polite language.

Does God care if we have good manners? Yes, he does. We learn in the Bible that God's people are to live their lives in a respectful and pleasing way so that others will think well of them. If we call ourselves Christians, it is important that our lives are lived in a way that honors God (Colossians 1:10).

There is no commandment in the Bible that says, "Have good manners and use the word "please," but the Bible does say, as you see on your paper: *"Let your speech always be gracious ..." (Colossians 4:6a). What does that mean? It means that when we talk we should use words that are kind, courteous, sweet, and pleasing. In 1 Corinthians 10:31 we read, "So, whether you eat or drink, or whatever you do, do everything for the glory of God." We need to think about what we say and do. Does it please and honor God? Can others see good things in us? How would Jesus feel about it?

Can we remember to have good manners? I hope so. Let's try.

*Use visual aid

Bossy Tigers
Jesus asks us to treat others like we want them to treat us.

Scripture: Matthew 7:12; Romans 12:10

Visual Aid: Use the coloring side of the activity page

Advance Preparations: Copy enough activity pages for each child to have one and have them ready to hand out.

The Sermon:
(*Hand out the activity pages, coloring side up.*) Are you ready for another rhyme? There is one on your paper, but first I have a question for you. Do you know what it means to be bossy? If someone is bossy they tell others what to do. Sometimes they are not nice about it. Now, I'm not talking about working for someone who is the boss. I am not talking about your teacher. She is trying to help you learn. I am not talking about your mom or dad either. If Mom or Dad seems to be bossy, it is because they are trying their best to take care of you. I am talking about those your age or near your age, children you know. Let's look at the picture and read what it says.

> **Each of the tigers thinks he is the boss.*
> *Why does that make the others so cross?*

When you are playing house, has anyone ever said, "I'm the mother. You're the kid?" Or have you ever tried to play a game of ball and someone insists they'll pitch and you have to go play in the field? Or maybe someone decides what you'll play and you don't get a chance to play what you'd like at all?

I think maybe this paper is not about tigers at all, but it is about you and me and people we know. Let's read some more:

> **It's no fun to work or play*
> *With someone who* must *have their way.*

Why would anyone be bossy? Could it be that a bossy person thinks his/her ideas or plans are better than anyone else's, or is it because the bossy person is just selfish, wanting his/her own way all the time? Let's read:

> **If we take turns and if we share*
> *And no one tries to be boss,*
> *If we treat others with love and care*
> *No one will likely be cross.*

No one likes a bossy person, but we must try to get alone with him or her anyway. Let us be careful that we are never bossy. There is a little Bible verse on your paper that is a good rule to follow: "In everything do to others as you would have them do to you ..." (Matthew 7:12). That means we treat others just like we want to be treated. Can you do that? I hope so. Let's try.

*Use visual aid

Messy Raccoons
Jesus asks us to say only good things about others.

Scripture: Psalm 141:3; James 3:2-12; Psalm 19:14

Visual Aid: Use the coloring side of the activity page

Advance Preparations: Copy enough activity pages for each child to have one and have them ready to hand out.

The Sermon:
(*Hand out the activity pages, coloring side up.*) We've been reading funny rhyming words for the past few weeks about animals. But, I don't think they're really about animals. I think they are about boys and girls and moms and dads. Here is a new one. Let's read it.

> **Raccoons got in the garbage,*
> *And spread it all around.*
> *I wonder why they did that.*
> *I wonder what they found.*

Sometimes people who live in the country or at the edge of a town will have raccoons living close by. A raccoon likes to get into a garbage can and spread the trash all around. Why would raccoons behave in such a way? Raccoons are animals, and animals behave like animals. But let's talk about people.

> **Why do we like tattling tales,*
> *Or spreading gossip dirt?*
> *That's worse than garbage on the ground,*
> *Because someone gets hurt.*

Here is something we all need to be careful about. Why do we tell things? Is it to get someone in trouble? Is it to make fun of someone? Is it to make ourselves look better than them? Do we just enjoy hearing and telling bad things? Why do we tell things?

Telling things could be to spread something good. We might tell how good someone is, what a good thing he or she did. Or, we might tell something to help. Like perhaps, the baby has climbed too high and might get hurt. Mom needs to come quick! Or baby is getting into something dangerous. In those cases, we need to tell. Or maybe someone has a problem and needs our prayers. That would be something good to tell.

When we begin to talk about someone, stop! Ask ourselves, is it true? Is it necessary? Is it kind? Will it help? Or will it hurt?

The Bible tells us in the book of James that it is very hard to remember to watch what we say, but we must try. God will help us if we'll ask. Psalm 141:3 is there on your paper. Let's read it: *"Set a guard over my mouth, O Lord; keep watch over the door of my lips." Can we do it? Let's try.

*Use visual aid

Crowing Roosters
Jesus asks us to be humble.

Scripture: Philippians 2:3b; Matthew 20:28; Galatians 5:26

Visual Aid: Use the coloring side of the activity page

Advance Preparations: Copy enough activity pages for each child to have one and have them ready to hand out.

The Sermon:
(*Hand out the activity pages, coloring side up.*) We have a rhyme on our paper again. Are you ready?

*A rooster will strut,
And he will crow.
Does that sound
Like someone you know?

A crowing rooster
Is okay.
He's just glad
To see a new day.

This talks about roosters, but I think it's really talking about boys and girls. Listen to this:

*Roosters are made
To crow a lot,
But boys and girls
Really are not.

Have you ever seen a rooster? He walks with a kind of strut. Have you ever heard one crow? It's loud!

When we talk about people crowing, what we mean is that they like to brag. Do you know anyone who likes to brag? What is bragging? It is talking about ourselves. It is telling how good we are or how smart we are. Maybe we brag about what we own or about how good we are at something like sports. It seems that no matter what it is, a person who brags is always better or best. Sometimes moms and dads will do this too. Sometimes grandparents brag about their grandchildren! Well, do you think maybe that's okay?

It is all right for us to know we can do something well. We need to believe in ourselves. But the problem comes when we compare ourselves with others. If we look at others and think we are better than they are, this is wrong. It might even cause us to talk about the others and put them down or laugh and make fun of them.

God wants us to be humble. If we are humble, we never, ever think we are better than others. All we have, all we are, has come from God. Yes, maybe we have worked hard or practiced hard to get good at something, but it is still God who has given us bodies and abilities and opportunities. What is there to brag about if all we have has come from God?

There's a verse from the Bible there on your paper: *"... In all humility regard others as better than yourselves" (Philippians 2:3).

Even Jesus who was God's very own son was humble. He willingly left his beautiful home in heaven to come to earth as a servant, serving us by dying for us (Matthew 20:28). If even Jesus was humble, we can be humble too. Let's try.

*Use visual aid

Buggy Thinking
Jesus asks us to think good thoughts.

Scripture: Psalm 139:23-24; Philippians 2:5; Colossians 3:2; Proverbs 12:5a

Visual Aid: Use the coloring side of the activity page

Advance Preparations: Copy enough activity pages for each child to have one and have them ready to hand out.

The Sermon:
(*Hand out the activity pages, coloring side up.*) Let's take a look at what our rhyme is for today:

**Is a bug in a rug
Really smug?*

*I don't know
And I don't care.
I'm gonna get him
Out of there.*

Do you like bugs? Some people called entomologists like to study bugs. One thing I'm sure of, no one, even an entomologist, likes bugs running around in their house. So we work to get rid of them. But what does the rest of our rhyme say?

*If a thing has bugs,
It's not working just right.
Let's get rid of those bugs.
Get 'em out of sight!*

Sometimes if something is working or running, but not quite right, we'll say that it has a few bugs in it. We mean that it needs to be fixed. We don't give up. We keep trying until we find what is wrong and fix it to make it right. We get rid of the bugs and it runs smoothly.

Sometimes, I'm afraid, we have bugs in our thinking. Our thoughts are not quite right. Our thoughts need to be fixed. Psalm 139:23-24 tells us we need to ask God for help: "Search me, O God, and know my heart; test me and know my *thoughts*. See if there is any hurtful[1] way in me, and lead me in the way everlasting."

What kind of thoughts have bugs and need to be fixed? There are many. Here are some examples. "All rich people are snobs." or "All poor people are dirty or thieves." Is that right? *No!* That's buggy thinking. How about this? "Nobody will ever know that I stole that candy." Buggy thinking again. Jesus knows. Or maybe we did something wrong and we say, "What I did wasn't as bad what some other people do." Buggy thinking, because if something is wrong, it's wrong no matter who does it.

We don't always know just how we should think. That's one reason it's important to know what the Bible says. We need to read it. That is why we should come to Sunday school and church regularly to hear the Bible taught and preached. This is how we learn what Jesus was like, what he thought, and what he taught.

There are many ways to have some bugs in our thoughts. How can we get rid of them? The Bible says we should have the mind of Christ: "Let the same mind be in you that was in Christ Jesus" (Philippians 2:5). We follow the example of Jesus. We try to think as he does, with love. There is no room in our thoughts for bugs if our thinking is filled with love both for Jesus and for one another.

It isn't easy, but let's work on it. Jesus will help.

*Use visual aid

---

1. The NRSV Bible uses the word "wicked," but has "hurtful" in the footnotes.

Funny Looking Animals
Jesus wants us to accept others no matter how they look.

Scripture: Galatians 3:26-29; Colossians 3:10-11; James 2; Ephesians 2:14-15

Visual Aid: Use the coloring side of the activity page

Advance Preparations: Copy enough activity pages for each child to have one and have them ready to hand out.

The Sermon:
(*Hand out the activity pages coloring side up.*) Today is the last day we'll have a paper with funny rhyming words. Let's read what it says:

> **A hippopotamus is too fat.*
> *A giraffe is way too tall.*
> *An elephant's nose is much too long,*
> *His ears too big, his eyes too small.*
> *And none of their colors suits me at all!*

Do you like animals? Have you ever been to a zoo? If you see a hippopotamus, do you think he's too fat? Do you think the giraffe is too tall and skinny? Do you look at an elephant and think it's surely ugly with such a big nose?

We don't think anything like that at all. We probably think how God has filled our earth with interesting animals and we enjoy each one. Let's read again from our paper:

> **God has made all living things.*
> *It's awesome, what he's done.*
> *We accept all God has made.*
> *There's beauty in each one.*

And yet, I'm afraid sometimes people don't treat each other in this kindly way. People look at someone and say they're too fat, they're too skinny, their ears are too big, their skin is a different color, they come from a different country, they speak a different language. Sometimes someone even makes fun of them.

How someone looks is not very important. What counts is, what kind of person he/she is. What does the Bible say? It's there on your paper: *"For in Christ Jesus you are all children of God through faith" (Galatians 3:26). All of us then, are children of God through faith in Jesus. We are made by him and he loves us all.

Colossians 3:10-11 plainly tells us that when we know Jesus as our Lord, all the things that separate people from people should be gone. Everyone loves and accepts everyone.

In James 2 the Bible tells us not to pay attention to how people look or how rich they are, but to treat everyone in a kind way.

Can we do this? I hope so. I'm going to try, are you?

*Use visual aid

If a mule says, "I won't do
Anything you want me to,"
Should I hit him or kick him,
Make faces and shout?
Should I pinch him, or trip him,
Or sit down and pout?

None of those things.
We can't make him do
Anything unless
He chooses to.

For God so loved the world that he gave his only Son, so that everyone who believes in him may not perish but may have eternal life.

— John 3:16

Some words from the Bible:
"... I have set before you life and death ... Choose life ... loving the Lord your God, obeying him, and holding fast to him...."
— Deuteronomy 30:19-20

"For God so loved the world that he gave his only Son, so that everyone who believes in him may not perish but may have eternal life." — John 3:16

Use the words from Deuteronomy and John to fill in the blanks.

I have set before you _ _ _ _ and _ _ _ _ _. _ _ _ _ _ _ life ... loving the _ _ _ _ your God, _ _ _ _ _ _ _ _ him and holding _ _ _ _ to him. We choose life when we accept Jesus as our Lord. God loves us so much that he _ _ _ _ his _ _ _ _ Son. _ _ _ _ _ _ _ _ _ _ who believes in Jesus will have _ _ _ _ _ _ _ life. That means a good happy life now and forever!

Find the words in the list. They go left to right or down.

N	L	A	S	A	V	I	O	R	X	E
O	I	A	E	M	I	T	W	X	A	T
W	F	S	T	U	B	B	O	R	N	E
F	E	K	X	L	E	D	N	J	Y	R
O	L	O	V	E	F	O	T	E	T	N
R	O	B	E	Y	O	U	G	S	H	A
E	M	E	T	O	R	Y	O	U	I	L
V	X	L	I	F	E	X	O	S	N	X
E	C	H	O	O	S	E	D	O	G	Y
R	X	A	B	U	N	D	A	N	T	E
T	H	I	N	K	D	E	A	T	H	S

STUBBORN THINK
AS CHOOSE
MULE LIFE
WON'T LOVE
DO OBEY
ANYTHING JESUS
YOU SAVIOR
ASK GOOD
ME ABUNDANT
TO NOW
SET ETERNAL
LIFE FOREVER
DEATH YES
BEFORE DO
YOU IT

Help the mule find its way to the stack of hay.

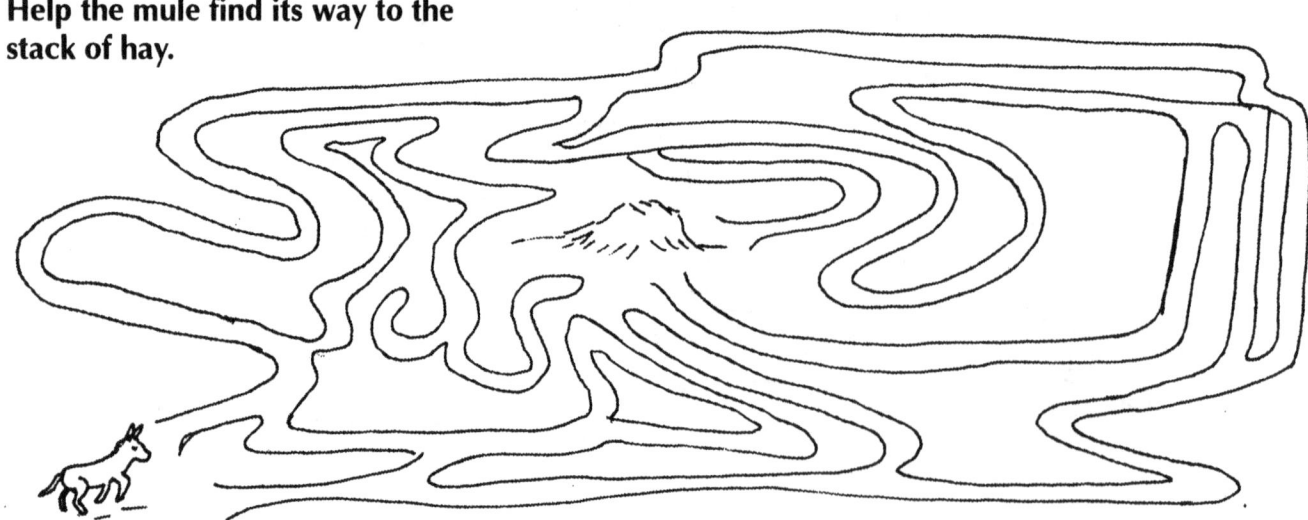

16

A soft answer
   turns away wrath,
But a harsh word
   stirs up anger.
         — Proverbs 15:1

If a lion
Wants to roar,
Should we
Let it in the door?

Roaring's like a bad disease.
Anyone can hatch it.
It spreads throughout the whole household.
Be careful or you'll catch it.

If you roar at me,
   I'll roar at you.
We'll wake the baby,
   And she roars too.

Then Mom comes to see.
   She adds her roars.
Oh, we should have kept
   That lion outdoors!

Here's what the Bible says:

"But now you must get rid of all such things — anger, wrath, malice, slander, and abusive language from your mouth." — Colossians 3:8

"A soft answer turns away wrath, but a harsh word stirs up anger." — Proverbs 15:1

Draw a line from each word to its meaning.

1. anger
2. wrath
3. malice
4. slander
5. abusive language
6. mouth
7. soft
8. answer
9. turns
10. stirs up

saying harmful things about someone
insulting language
opening used for talking
makes it worse
to change around
an unfriendly feeling
a very unfriendly feeling
a desire to harm
kind and gentle
a reply

Read the scripture verses. What does the Bible say to do about the first five words in the activity to the left? Cross out six wrong answers in the phrases below.

keep it up
do something worse back
don't admit it
get rid of it all
answer with harsh words
give a soft answer
yell back
get even

Find the words in the list. They go left to right or down.

```
G E T W O R D S C X A
A S O F T Y O U O S N
B I M P O R T A N T G
O F E E L I N G C N E
U S E L F I S H E P R
T R Y O U R O A R S H
R D B W H A T X N X E
I W A N T B E Y E L L
D C A R E F U L D X P
T H I N G S J E S U S
L I O N S P R E A D S
```

SELFISH
CONCERNED
OUR
OWN
FEELING
WHAT
WANT
IMPORTANT
TO
ME
ROAR
YELL
ABOUT
THINGS
BE

CAREFUL
SPREADS
GET
RID
LION
TO
USE
SOFT
WORDS
ANGER
JESUS
HELPS
YOU
DO
TRY

There are 12 mouths hidden in this picture. Can you find them?

Should monkeys scream for ice cream?

There is a word, "PLEASE"
And if they'll use it,
I doubt if anyone
Will refuse it.

Let your speech
always be gracious....
— Colossians 4:6a

Here is something from the Bible:
"So whether you eat or drink, or whatever you do, do everything for the glory of God. Give no offense...."
— 1 Corinthians 10:31-32a

"Let your speech always be gracious...."
— Colossians 4:6a

Untangle the words that are in the sentences below each space, then write them correctly in the space. See the list of words for help.

We are _____, God's _____, so we _____
        iasnChsitr   ppoele   loudsh

always _____ in a _____ and _____ way.
       cta   gnisaelp   pectresful

_____ we ___ should be _____ in a _____ that
  inthgvrEey   od   eodn   ayw

_____ God. Our _____ should always be _____,
  oohrsn   eehcps   cgarouis

kind and _____. God wants us to have good manners.
         tleeng

speech	should
gentle	way
Christians	pleasing
people	respectful
do	honors
done	gracious
act	Everything

Find the words in the list. They go left to right or down.

```
L A N G U A G E O R
G I R L S X X V X P
P L I K E X W E D O
L G X B A N D R X L
E O M O N K E Y S I
A D X Y O U X T M T
S Y E S N O T H A E
E S C R E A M I N G
H S H O U L D N N O
E X D R I N K G E O
L A S K H O N O R D
P X A N I M A L S I
K N O W J E S U S T
T R Y E A T H A N K
```

SCREAMING	WE
MONKEYS	DO
SHOULD	EAT
USE	OR
POLITE	DRINK
LANGUAGE	YES
LIKE	GOOD
PLEASE	MANNERS
AND	HONOR
THANK	GOD
YOU	KNOW
NOT	ASK
ANIMALS	JESUS
BOYS	HELP
GIRLS	TRY
EVERYTHING	IT

20

Each of the tigers
Thinks he is the boss.
Why does that make
The others so cross?

It's no fun
To work or play
With someone who
Must have their way.

In everything do to
others as you would
have them do to you....
— Matthew 7:12

If we take turns
  and if we share
And no one tries
  to be boss,
If we treat others
  with love and care
No one will likely
  be cross.

If I have to be nice to others,
Does that include my sisters and brothers?

**Find the words in the list.
They go left to right or down.**

B	O	S	S	Y	L	O	V	E	D
W	P	E	O	P	L	E	S	W	O
H	T	O	M	A	R	E	H	E	X
A	F	F	E	C	T	I	O	N	T
T	T	I	G	E	R	S	W	X	H
O	H	W	A	N	T	L	I	K	E
T	E	L	L	W	E	X	N	B	M
H	Y	H	O	N	O	R	G	E	U
E	M	U	S	T	R	E	A	T	T
R	T	R	E	A	T	E	D	X	U
S	C	A	R	E	H	E	L	P	A
J	E	S	U	S	D	O	I	T	L

SOME   DO   MUTUAL
PEOPLE   WE   AFFECTION
ARE   MUST   SHOWING
TIGERS   TREAT   HONOR
BOSSY   THEM   LOVE
THEY   LIKE   CARE
TELL   WE   DO
OTHERS   WANT   IT
WHAT   BE   JESUS
TO   TREATED   HELP

This is what the Bible says:
"In everything do to others as you would have them do to you...."   — Matthew 7:12

"Love one another with mutual affection; outdo one another in showing honor."
— Romans 12:10

We are all to love each other, sharing with others tender feelings and trying to do better than anyone else in showing great respect for each one.

Draw a line from each word to its meaning.

outdo   to put in sight
mutual   sharing with others
affection   to do better
honor   tender feeling
showing   to respect greatly

Finish the tiger then give him stripes.

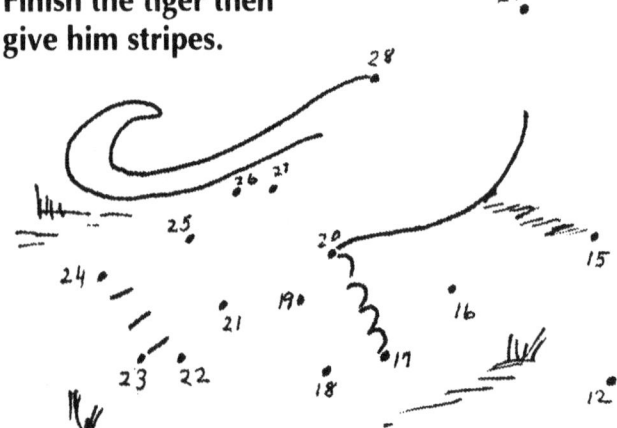

Raccoons got in the garbage
And spread it all around.
I wonder why they did that.
I wonder what they found.

Why do we like tattling tales,
Or spreading gossip dirt?
That's worse than garbage on the ground,
Because someone gets hurt.

Set a guard over my mouth O Lord;
Keep watch over the door of my lips.
— Psalm 141:3

What does the Bible say?

"Set a guard over my mouth, O Lord; keep watch over the door of my lips."
— Psalm 141:3

"Let the words of my mouth and the meditation of my heart be acceptable to you O Lord, my rock and my redeemer."
— Psalm 19:14

What do the words in these verses mean? Draw a line from each word to its meaning.

guard	to think deeply
watch	a firm support
door	to watch and keep from trouble
words	a movable opening
meditation	a deliverer from sin
acceptable	careful guarding
rock	speech
redeemer	to approve

Find a word from the list that will make sense in the blanks.

Raccoons will spread _ _ _ _ _ _ _ around if they get a chance. Animals can only act like _ _ _ _ _ _ _. People _ _ _ _ _ _ know better. Telling hurtful things about others is called _ _ _ _ _ _. We should be _ _ _ _ _ _ _ to tell only good things. We want to _ _ _ _ _ not _ _ _ _ _ others by what we _ _ _. We can ask ourselves, is it _ _ _ _ _ _ _ _ _ _? Is it _ _ _ _ _? We can ask God to set a _ _ _ _ _ _ and keep _ _ _ _ _ over our mouths.

necessary
garbage
watch
animals
guard
should
kind
gossip
say
careful
hurt
help

Find the words in the list. They go left to right or down.

S	P	R	E	A	D	I	N	G	Y
C	G	A	N	I	M	A	L	O	E
A	A	C	H	U	R	T	S	S	S
R	R	C	X	W	O	R	D	S	D
E	B	O	K	I	N	D	X	I	O
F	A	O	W	A	T	C	H	P	I
U	G	N	G	U	A	R	D	B	T
L	E	S	A	Y	L	I	K	E	X

RACCOONS   HURTS   GUARD
ANIMAL   BE   WATCH
GARBAGE   CAREFUL   YES
LIKE   SAY   DO
SPREADING KIND   IT
GOSSIP   WORDS

The raccoon is looking for 20 apples. Can you help him find them?

A rooster will strut
And he will crow.
Does that sound
Like someone you know?

A crowing rooster
Is okay.
He's just glad
To see a new day.

Roosters are made
To crow a lot,
But boys and girls
Really are not.

... in humility regard others as
better than yourselves.
— Philippians 2:3b

Find the words in the list. They go left to right or down.

```
X C O N C E I T E D E
C O N F I D E N T I N
G O C R O W B O D Y V
O P P O R T U N I T Y
D P X M B S E R V E D
C O M P E T E L O V E
H S E L F I S H B U T
U I A B I L I T I E S
M T R E G A R D O J G
B I E O T H E R S E I
L O D X O R B E W S V
E N O T B R A G E U E
B E T T E R Y E S S N
```

BE	ENVY	ABILITIES
CONFIDENT	COMPETE	OPPORTUNITY
BUT	IN	FROM
DO	OPPOSITION	GOD
NOT	REGARD	LOVE
CROW	OTHERS	HUMBLE
BRAG	BETTER	SERVED
OR	WE	US
BE	ARE	YES
CONCEITED	GIVEN	JESUS
SELFISH	BODY	

Read what the Bible says:

"Do nothing from selfish ambition or conceit, but in humility regard others as better than yourselves." — Philippians 2:3

"Let us not become conceited, competing against one another, envying one another." — Galatians 5:26

Complete the words with the vowels a e i o u.

R__ __st __rs are supposed to cr__w. If p__ __pl__ crow, that means that they br__g. The B__bl__ t__lls us we should b__ h__mbl__. If we are humble, we w__ll not th__nk of ours__lv__s as b__tt__r th__n others. All w__ h__ve or __r__ has b__ __n g__v__n t__ us fr__m God. So what is there to brag about? Jesus was humble. He c__m__ t__ __ __rth as a servant. He s__rv__d us by dy__ng on the cr__ss for us __ll.

As the rooster finds its path, pick up each letter and write them in the blanks.

_ _ _ _ _   _ _ _

_ _ _

_ _

26

Is a bug in a rug
Really snug?

I don't know
And I don't care.
I'm gonna get him
Out of there.

If a thing has bugs,
It's not working just right.
Let's get rid of those bugs.
Get 'em all out of sight!

Search me, O God and know my heart;
test me and know my *thoughts*.
See if there is any hurtful way in me,
and lead me in the way everlasting.
— Psalm 139:23-24

Let's read what the Bible says:
"Search me, O God, and know my heart; test me and know my thoughts. See if there is any hurtful way in me, and lead me in the way everlasting."
— Psalm 139:23-24

"Let the same mind be in you that was in Christ Jesus." — Philippians 2:5

Find the words in the list. They go left to right or down.

R	U	G	A	B	O	V	E	X	B
L	O	V	E	X	B	W	A	Y	U
S	N	U	G	B	U	T	R	X	G
X	T	H	O	U	G	H	T	S	I
G	E	T	O	G	G	I	H	E	T
M	I	N	D	S	Y	N	X	A	T
R	I	D	W	O	R	K	S	R	H
H	E	A	R	T	F	I	X	C	E
A	N	D	W	R	O	N	G	H	O
K	N	O	W	R	I	G	H	T	F
M	E	T	H	I	N	K	X	M	Y

BUG   SEARCH
SNUG   ME
IN   KNOW
THE   MY
RUG   HEART
GET   FIX
RID   THINK
OF   RIGHT
BUGS   WAY
AND   EARTH
BUGGY   WRONG
THINKING   GOOD
MINDS   WORKS
THOUGHTS   LOVE
ABOVE

There is a good Bible verse from Colossians 3:2:
"Set your minds on things that are above, not on things that are on earth...."

If we set our minds on heavenly things, what kind of thoughts will be in our minds? Circle the good thoughts. Draw a line from a bad thought to a bug.

I hate him!
I'll invite him to Sunday school.
She looks stupid.
She has a nice smile.
I'm going to laugh at his big feet.
He's got nice manners.
Mom said, "No," but I will anyway.
If Mom said, "No," then I won't.
No one will see me take it.
I'll save my money and buy it.
I'll never forgive her.
I hope she feels better tomorrow.
She is not good enough to come to my party.
I want everyone at my party.
Mom looks tired, maybe I can help.

A hippopotamus is too fat.
A giraffe is way too tall.
An elephant's nose
 is much too long,
His ears too big,
 his eyes too small.
And none of their colors
 suits me at all.

God has made all
 living things.
It's awesome, what
 he's done.
We accept all God
 has made.
There's beauty in
 each one.

For in Christ Jesus
you are all children
of God through faith.
 — Galatians 3:26

Find the words in the list. They go left to right or down.

H	G	E	T	S	W	T	W	E	J	D	M
O	K	S	E	P	A	R	A	T	E	I	A
W	I	T	H	E	L	E	N	H	S	V	T
T	N	T	L	O	L	A	D	A	U	I	T
H	D	H	O	P	S	T	X	N	S	D	E
I	L	E	O	L	O	V	I	N	G	I	R
N	Y	Y	K	E	M	L	I	K	E	N	M
G	T	M	O	R	E	T	H	A	T	G	U
S	O	H	O	S	T	I	L	I	T	Y	S
N	O	B	E	V	E	R	Y	O	N	E	T
R	I	D	B	U	T	O	T	H	E	R	S

WE	MATTER
LIKE	HOW
TO	THEY
BE	LOOK
WITH	LOVING
SOME	JESUS
PEOPLE	GETS
MORE	RID
THAN	THINGS
OTHERS	THAT
BUT	SEPARATE
MUST	HOSTILITY
TREAT	AND
EVERYONE	DIVIDING
KINDLY	WALLS
NO	

Draw a line from each word to its meaning.

peace — unfriendly feelings
flesh — discontinued or got rid of it
group — pleasing agreement
broken down — to treat some better than others
dividing wall — body
hostility — many who in some way are all alike
partiality — doing something wrong
sin — something that separates

Look at what the Bible says:

"For he [Jesus] is our peace; in his flesh he has made both groups into one and has broken down the dividing wall, that is, the hostility between us."   — Ephesians 2:14

"But if you show partiality, you commit sin...."
   — James 2:9a

Find the hidden letters in the animals to fill the blanks and make a sentence.

_ _ _ _ _ _ _ to

_ _ _ _ _ _ _ _ _.

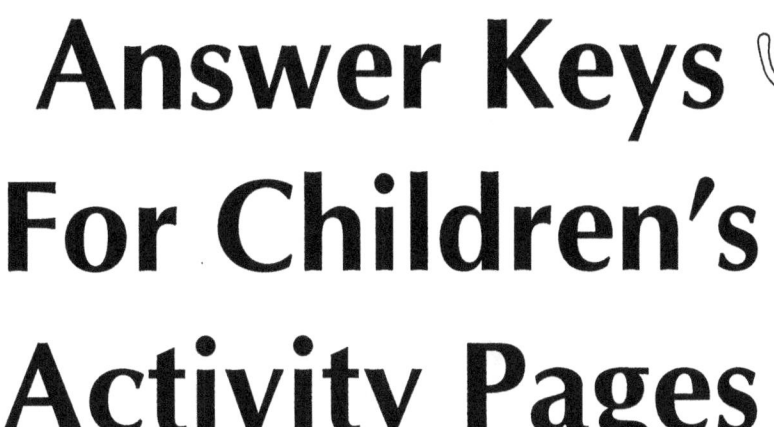

Answer Keys For Children's Activity Pages

ANSWER KEYS

Pages 16, 18, 20

Some words from the Bible:
"... I have set before you life and death ... Choose life ... loving the Lord your God, obeying him, and holding fast to him..."
— Deuteronomy 30:19-20

"For God so loved the world that he gave his only Son, so that everyone who believes in him may not perish but may have eternal life."
— John 3:16

Use the words from Deuteronomy and John to fill in the blanks.

I have set before you **l i f e** and **d e a t h**. **C h o o s e** life ... loving the **L o r d** your God, **o b e y i n g** him and holding **f a s t** to him. We choose life when we accept Jesus as our Lord. God loves us so much that he **g a v e** his **o n l y** Son. **E v e r y o n e** who believes in Jesus will have **e t e r n a l** life. That means a good happy life now and forever!

Find the words in the list. They go left to right or down.

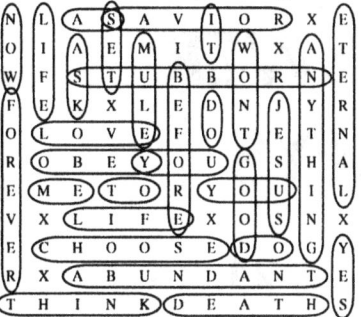

STUBBORN	THINK
AS	CHOOSE
MULE	LIFE
WON'T	LOVE
DO	OBEY
ANYTHING	JESUS
YOU	SAVIOR
ASK	GOOD
ME	ABUNDANT
TO	NOW
SET	ETERNAL
LIFE	FOREVER
DEATH	YES
BEFORE	DO
YOU	IT

Help the mule find its way to the stack of hay.

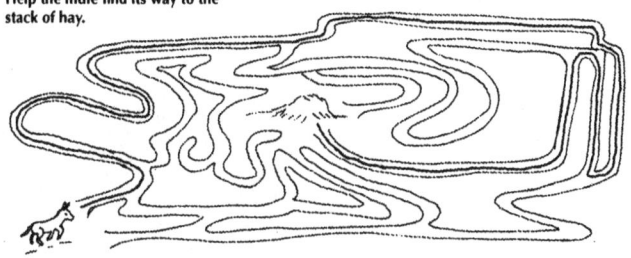

Here's what the Bible says:
"But now you must get rid of all such things — anger, wrath, malice, slander, and abusive language from your mouth."
— Colossians 3:8

Draw a line from each word to its meaning.

1. anger — a very unfriendly feeling
2. wrath — insulting language
3. malice — a desire to harm
4. slander — saying harmful things about someone
5. abusive language — makes it worse
6. mouth — opening used for talking
7. soft — kind and gentle
8. answer — a reply
9. turns — to change around
10. stirs up — an unfriendly feeling

"A soft answer turns away wrath, but a harsh word stirs up anger."
— Proverbs 15:1

Read the scripture verses. What does the Bible say to do about the first five words in the activity to the left? Cross out six wrong answers in the phrases below.

~~keep it up~~
~~do something worse back~~
~~don't admit it~~
get rid of it all
~~answer with harsh words~~
give a soft answer
~~yell back~~
~~get even~~

Find the words in the list. They go left to right or down.

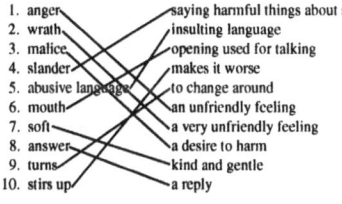

SELFISH	CAREFUL
CONCERNED	SPREADS
OUR	GET
OWN	RID
FEELING	LION
WHAT	TO
WANT	USE
IMPORTANT	SOFT
TO	WORDS
ME	ANGER
ROAR	JESUS
YELL	HELPS
ABOUT	YOU
THINGS	DO
BE	TRY

There are 12 mouths hidden in this picture. Can you find them?

Here is something from the Bible:
"So whether you eat or drink, or whatever you do, do everything for the glory of God. Give no offense...."
— 1 Corinthians 10:31-32a

"Let your speech always be gracious...."
— Colossians 4:6a

Untangle the words that are in the sentences below each space, then write them correctly in the space. See the list of words for help.

We are **Christians**, God's **people**, so we **should**
       iasnChsitr   ppoele   loudsh
always **act** in a **pleasing** and **respectful** way.
        cta   gnisaelp   pectresful
Everything we **do** should be **done** in a **way** that
 inthgvrEey   od   codn   ayw
honors God. Our **speech** should always be **gracious**,
 oohrsn   eehcps   cgarouis
kind and **gentle**. God wants us to have good manners.
          tleeng

speech	should
gentle	way
Christians	pleasing
people	respectful
do	honors
done	gracious
act	Everything

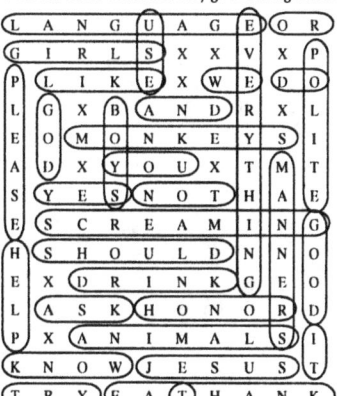

Find the words in the list. They go left to right or down.

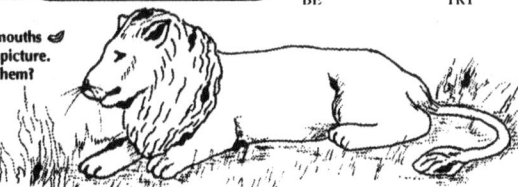

SCREAMING	WE
MONKEYS	DO
SHOULD	EAT
USE	OR
POLITE	DRINK
LANGUAGE	YES
LIKE	GOOD
PLEASE	MANNERS
AND	HONOR
THANK	GOD
YOU	KNOW
NOT	ASK
ANIMALS	JESUS
BOYS	HELP
GIRLS	TRY
EVERYTHING	IT

33

ANSWER KEYS

Pages 22, 24, 26

Find the words in the list. They go left to right or down.

```
B O S S Y L O V E D
W P E O P L E S W O
H T O M A R E H X
A F F E C T I O N T
T T I G E R S W X H
O H W A N T L I K E
T E L L W E X N B M
H Y H O N O R G E U
E M U S T R E A T T
R T R E A T E D X U
S C A R E H E L P A
J E S U S D O I T L
```

SOME	DO	MUTUAL
PEOPLE	WE	AFFECTION
ARE	MUST	SHOWING
TIGERS	TREAT	HONOR
BOSSY	THEM	LOVE
THEY	LIKE	CARE
TELL	WE	DO
OTHERS	WANT	IT
WHAT	BE	JESUS
TO	TREATED	HELP

This is what the Bible says:

"In everything do to others as you would have them do to you...."
— Matthew 7:12

"Love one another with mutual affection; outdo one another in showing honor."
— Romans 12:10

We are all to love each other, sharing with others tender feelings and trying to do better than anyone else in showing great respect for each one.

Draw a line from each word to its meaning.

outdo — to do better
mutual — sharing with others
affection — tender feeling
honor — to respect greatly
showing — to put in sight

Finish the tiger then give him stripes.

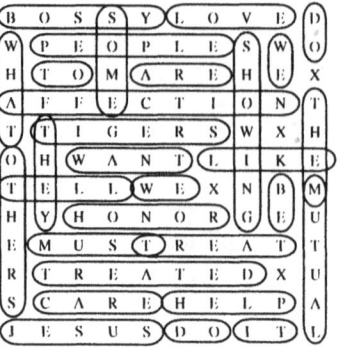

What does the Bible say?

"Set a guard over my mouth, O Lord; keep watch over the door of my lips."
— Psalm 141:3

"Let the words of my mouth and the meditation of my heart be acceptable to you O Lord, my rock and my redeemer."
— Psalm 19:14

What do the words in these verses mean? Draw a line from each word to its meaning.

guard — careful guarding
watch — to watch and keep from trouble
door — a movable opening
words — speech
meditation — to think deeply
acceptable — to approve
rock — a firm support
redeemer — a deliverer from sin

Find a word from the list that will make sense in the blanks.

Raccoons will spread **g a r b a g e** around if they get a chance. Animals can only act like **a n i m a l s**. People **s h o u l d** know better. Telling hurtful things about others is called **g o s s i p**. We should be **c a r e f u l** to tell only good things. We want to **h e l p** not **h u r t** others by what we **s a y**. We can ask ourselves, is it **n e c e s s a r y**? Is it **k i n d**? We can ask God to set a **w a t c h** and keep **g u a r d** over our mouths.

necessary
garbage
watch
animals
guard
should
kind
gossip
say
careful
hurt
help

Find the words in the list. They go left to right or down.

```
S P R E A D I N G Y
C A N I M A L O E
A G C H U R T S S
R R X W O R D S
E B K I N D X I
F A W A T C H P
U G N G U A R D B
L E S A Y L I K E X
```

RACCOONS	HURTS	GUARD
ANIMAL	BE	WATCH
GARBAGE	CAREFUL	YES
LIKE	SAY	DO
SPREADING	KIND	IT
GOSSIP	WORDS	

The raccoon is looking for 20 apples. Can you help him find them?

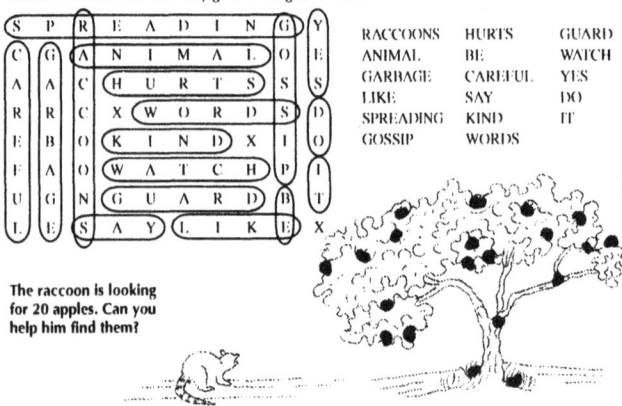

Find the words in the list. They go left to right or down.

```
X C O N C E I T E D E
C O N F I D E N T I N
G O C R O W B O D Y V
O P P O R T U N I T Y
D P X M B S E R V E D
C O M P E T E L O V E
H S E L F I S H B U T
U A B I L I T I E S
M T R E G A R D O
B I O T H E R S J
L O X O R B E W I V
E N O T B R A G U E
B E T T E R Y E S
```

BE	ENVY	ABILITIES
CONFIDENT	COMPETE	OPPORTUNITY
BUT	IN	FROM
DO	OPPOSITION	GOD
NOT	REGARD	LOVE
CROW	OTHERS	HUMBLE
BRAG	BETTER	SERVED
OR	WE	US
BE	ARE	YES
CONCEITED	GIVEN	JESUS
SELFISH	BODY	

Read what the Bible says:

"Do nothing from selfish ambition or conceit, but in humility regard others as better than yourselves."
— Philippians 2:3

"Let us not become conceited, competing against one another, envying one another."
— Galatians 5:26

Complete the words with the vowels a e i o u.

R**oo** **o**st**e**rs are supposed to cr**ow**. If p**eo**pl**e** crow, that means that they br**a**g. The B**i**bl**e** t**e**lls us we should b**e** h**u**mbl**e**. If we are humble, we w**i**ll not th**i**nk of ours**e**lves as b**e**tt**e**r th**a**n others. All w**e** h**a**ve or **a**re has b**ee**n g**i**v**e**n t**o** us fr**o**m God. So what is there to brag about? Jesus was humble. He c**a**me t**o** **e**arth as a servant. He s**e**rv**e**d us by dy**i**ng on the cr**o**ss for us **a**ll.

As the rooster finds its path, pick up each letter and write them in the blanks.

J e s u s   d i e d
f o r
u s

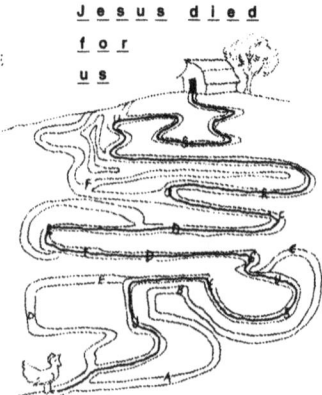

34

ANSWER KEYS

Pages 28, 30

Let's read what the Bible says:
"Search me, O God, and know my heart; test me and know my thoughts. See if there is any hurtful way in me, and lead me in the way everlasting."
— Psalm 139:23-24

"Let the same mind be in you that was in Christ Jesus." — Philippians 2:5

Find the words in the list. They go left to right or down.

BUG	SEARCH
SNUG	ME
IN	KNOW
THE	MY
RUG	HEART
GET	FIX
RID	THINK
OF	RIGHT
BUGS	WAY
AND	EARTH
BUGGY	WRONG
THINKING	GOOD
MINDS	WORKS
THOUGHTS	LOVE
ABOVE	

There is a good Bible verse from Colossians 3:2:
"Set your minds on things that are above, not on things that are on earth...."

If we set our minds on heavenly things, what kind of thoughts will be in our minds? Circle the good thoughts. Draw a line from a bad thought to a bug.

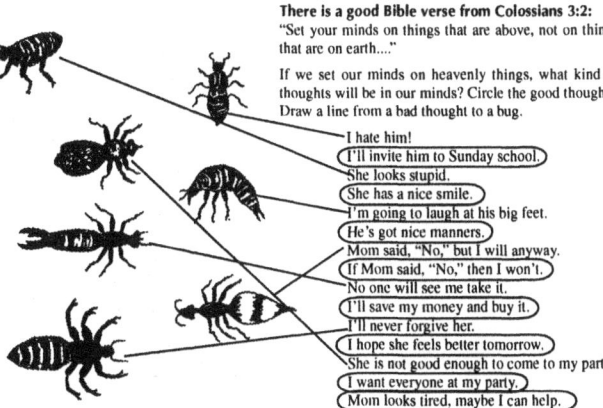

- I hate him!
- (I'll invite him to Sunday school.)
- She looks stupid.
- (She has a nice smile.)
- I'm going to laugh at his big feet.
- (He's got nice manners.)
- Mom said, "No," but I will anyway.
- (If Mom said, "No," then I won't.)
- No one will see me take it.
- (I'll save my money and buy it.)
- I'll never forgive her.
- (I hope she feels better tomorrow.)
- She is not good enough to come to my party.
- (I want everyone at my party.)
- (Mom looks tired, maybe I can help.)

Find the words in the list. They go left to right or down.

WE	MATTER
LIKE	HOW
TO	THEY
BE	LOOK
WITH	LOVING
SOME	JESUS
PEOPLE	GETS
MORE	RID
THAN	THINGS
OTHERS	THAT
BUT	SEPARATE
MUST	HOSTILITY
TREAT	AND
EVERYONE	DIVIDING
KINDLY	WALLS
NO	

Draw a line from each word to its meaning.

- peace — pleasing agreement
- flesh — body
- group — many who in some way are all alike
- broken down — discontinued or got rid of it
- dividing wall — something that separates
- hostility — unfriendly feelings
- partiality — to treat some better than others
- sin — doing something wrong

Look at what the Bible says:
"For he [Jesus] is our peace; in his flesh he has made both groups into one and has broken down the dividing wall, that is, the hostility between us." — Ephesians 2:14

"But if you show partiality, you commit sin...." — James 2:9a

Find the hidden letters in the animals to fill the blanks and make a sentence.

B e   k i n d to e v e r y o n e.

35

www.ingramcontent.com/pod-product-compliance
Lightning Source LLC
Chambersburg PA
CBHW081351040426
42450CB00015B/3400

9 780788 018091